LUNCH-HOUR LESSONS
Revelation

"A revealing of Jesus, the Messiah."
Revelation 1:1 THE MESSAGE

Linda Osborne

Copyright © 2013 Linda Osborne

All rights reserved.

Catch The Vision! Press

504 A Harbor View Drive, Klamath Falls, OR 97601

ISBN:-10: 0615862969
ISBN-13: 9780615862965

DEDICATION

To my Lord and Savior, Jesus Christ. The first and the last, the living one who was dead but is now alive forevermore!

CONTENTS

Preface	i
Getting Started	1
Revelation 1	2
Revelation 2	4
Revelation 3	7
Revelation 4	10
Revelation 5	13
Revelation 6	16
Revelation 7	19
Revelation 8	22
Revelation 9	25
Revelation 10	28
Revelation 11	31
Revelation 12	34
Revelation 13	37
Revelation 14	40
Revelation 15	43
Revelation 16	46
Revelation 17	49
Revelation 18	52
Revelation 19	55
Revelation 20	58
Revelation 21	61
Revelation 22	64
About the Author	67

PREFACE

I originally wrote this study in correlation with Hal Lindsey's book, *There's A New World Coming*. Although you can certainly do this study without that book, it is an amazing commentary on the book of Revelation, and you would benefit greatly by using it as a study aid as you work through this book which, being a prophetic book, can be somewhat difficult to interpret and understand. If you don't use Hal's commentary, you may want to read this book in the New Living Translation and/or find another good commentary to help you get more from your study.

What an amazing adventure we begin as we step into our study of the Book of Revelation, which promises a blessing to all who enter in! We will be looking into things which were previously closed to us but are now opening up to our understanding as the day draws near. We will have the opportunity, as we go through this exciting book, to consider the events of our own day, which are setting the stage for the prophecy of Revelation to unfold. Get a good seat, have your Bible and notebook ready, and let the adventures begin!

GETTING STARTED

It is always good to begin a study by looking at the book as a whole. You may, therefore, want to read this entire book in one sitting before you start your study verse by verse.

In each lesson of the study there will be two sets of questions. The first section is called *Just The Facts* and will focus on the Scripture passage at hand, virtually going through the chapter in a verse by verse manner. The second section is called *Making It Personal* and is designed for you to take the subject you're studying and share how it relates to you on a more personal and even interpretive level.

As in any study of the Bible, before you begin you should ask the Lord to open up the Scripture to you by the power of His Holy Spirit and to show you personally what He want wants you to see. Because this book of the Bible is particularly difficult—just do your best! Learn what you can and receive what you are able to. Even if you only scratch the surface, you will have more of this book at the end of this study than you did at the beginning!

> "He who has an ear, let him hear what the Spirit says to the churches." (Revelation 2:7)

REVELATION 1

Just The Facts!

READ REVELATION 1
1. What is the theme and purpose of this book? v. 1

2. What is promised to the student of the Book of Revelation? v. 3 What will this student do to receive this blessing?

3. To whom was this vision given? What do you know about him from your previous studies? What do you know about him from this chapter?

4. Who was this letter written to? v. 4

   a. With what symbol were these churches represented? Why might this have been? See vv. 12 and 20.

   b. Why do you think these particular churches may have been chosen to be the recipients of this letter of prophecy?

REVELATION 1

5. The Book of Revelation gives its own outline. What is it? v. 19

6. What does Jesus look like in this chapter? vv. 13-16

   a. Compare this picture to the one presented in Philippians 2:5-8 and Isaiah 53:2-3.

   b. What took place that makes the difference between the picture of Jesus in Isaiah and the one in Revelation 1?

Making It Personal

1. Share some of the things you have you learned about Jesus from your study of Revelation 1. (You may also see Colossians 1:15-18.)

2. What are you hoping to gain personally as you study this book?

REVELATION 2

The seven selected churches were located in the Roman province of Asia—actually Asia Minor, which today is Turkey. These seven churches were connected by a triangular highway and are named in their geographical order beginning with Ephesus, the most prominent, and going in a clockwise direction ending with Laodicea. Most likely this letter was carried along this same route and given out in the same order as it was written. John would have been well-known in this area, as he had spent much of his life and ministry in Ephesus.

This week we will look at the first four churches—Ephesus, Smyrna, Pergamos, and Thyatira.

Just The Facts!

READ REVELATION 2
As we look at the message given to each of the churches, let's remember that Jesus knew them intimately. He knew their struggles, He knew their successes, He knew their failures, He knew their affections, and He knew their motives.

1. What did He have to say:

To Ephesus (vv. 1-7)?

✣ Description of Jesus:

✣ Commendation:

✣ Rebuke:

✣ Promise to overcomers:

REVELATION 2

To Smyrna (vv. 8-11)?

✠ Description of Jesus:

✠ Commendation:

✠ Rebuke:

✠ Promise to overcomers:

To Pergamos (vv. 12-17)?

✠ Description of Jesus:

✠ Commendation:

✠ Rebuke:

✠ Promise to overcomers:

To Thyatira (vv. 18-29)?

✠ Description of Jesus:

✠ Commendation:

✠ Rebuke:

✣ Promise to overcomers:

2. Each letter speaks to the one who overcomes. Who is the overcomer according to 1 John 5:4-5?

Making It Personal

What would you think if you got a personal letter from Jesus? Well you have! These letters are for you! Now let's look at the first four letters from a personal perspective.

1. To which of these churches do you most relate?

2. Which of these letters ministered to you the most?

3. Did the Lord speak a word of commendation to you as you studied these letters?

4. Was there a word of rebuke?

5. Which description of Jesus speaks to you the most?

6. Which promise to these churches excites you the most?

REVELATION 3

Today we continue our study of the letters to the seven chosen churches. This week we will look at the final three churches—Sardis, to whom Jesus gives a wake-up call, Philadelphia, the second church which receives only commendation with no rebuke, and finally Laodicea, the church Jesus loves enough to reprove, and calls to repentance. Laodicea represents the time in the history of the church in which we are now living. Take heed!

Just The Facts!

READ REVELATION 3
Remember that the One who wrote these words knew the hearts, the motives, and the life situations of these churches intimately ...

1. What does Jesus have to say:

To Sardis (vv. 1-6)?

✢ Description of Jesus:

✢ Commendation:

✢ Rebuke:

✢ Promise to overcomers:

To Philadelphia (vv. 7-13)?

✢ Description of Jesus:

✢ Commendation:

✢ Rebuke:

✢ Promise to overcomers:

To Laodicea (vv. 14-22)?

✢ Description of Jesus:

✢ Commendation:

✢ Rebuke:

✢ Promise to overcomers:

Making It Personal

1. To which of these churches do you most relate?

2. Which of these letters ministered to you the most?

3. Did the Lord speak a word of commendation to you as you studied these letters?

REVELATION 3

4. Was there a word of rebuke?

5. Which description of Jesus speaks to you the most?

6. Which promise to these churches excites you the most?

7. What's one way to know if your church is spiritually alive? Equally so, how can you know if *you* are spiritually alive?

REVELATION 4

A door in heaven! The sound of a trumpet saying the words, "Come up here"! Thrones, jewels, lightening, thunder, and voices! Lamps of fire, a sea of glass, and four living creatures speaking words of praise as 24 elders cast their crowns! That is what we have before us this week!

Chapter 4 is the turning point in the Book of Revelation as it dramatically and excitingly takes us into the final section of the book. We remember the outline, as given in Revelation 1:19:

- 1st John was to write about the "things which you have seen." This was John's vision as recorded in Chapter 1.
- 2nd John was to write about the "things which are." These were the messages spoken by Jesus to the seven churches, as recorded in Chapters 2-3. This portion of the book pertains to the church age.
- 3rd John was to write about the "things which shall take place after these things." This is the message, recorded in chapters 4-22, of the things that will take place at the conclusion of church history.

Just The Facts!

READ REVELATION 4

1. *After these things* what did John see and what did he hear? v. 1

    a. What had happened to John? v. 2 Note how quickly this happened.

2. How did John describe the One he saw on the throne? v. 3 Is he describing His form? What is he describing?

REVELATION 4

3. Who was seated *around* the throne? v. 4

   a. What proceeded *from* the throne? v. 5

   b. What was *before* the throne? What does verse 5 say these are?

   c. What else did John see *before* the throne? v. 6

4. Describe the living creatures from verses 7 and 8.

   a. What do they continually say? What are they doing here?

   b. What also happens as they give glory to God? v. 10

Making It Personal

1. How is John's transference to heaven a picture of what will happen to us?

2. Share from these verses what exactly will take place: 1 Corinthians 15:51-52; 1 Thessalonians 4:15-17.

3. How exciting is it to realize that the church which was once pictured on this earth (Chapters 2-3) is now seated before God around the throne?

4. What understanding about the Rapture of the Church have you gained from studying this chapter?

REVELATION 5

In the Book of Leviticus, a law was given in which a man's land could be reclaimed by a kinsman-redeemer. If a man, in his poverty or for another reason, lost his right to his land, a family relative could "redeem" the land for him in order to keep it in the family. Because of the fact that the Lord God had given the land to Israel, keeping the land within its original family was extremely important. So important, in fact, that the transaction was written on a scroll and sealed seven times. On the day of the land's redemption, the scroll was finally able to be opened by the one who was qualified to redeem it. Can you even begin to imagine how blessed the poor relative was when his land was redeemed?

When Adam sinned he, in effect, forfeited his right of ownership of the earth to Satan. God didn't challenge the fact that Satan was the new, though temporary, ruler of the earth (see Job 1:6-7). Jesus didn't challenge the fact that Satan now controlled the earth (see Matthew 4:1-11). But, although not challenging it at the moment, a plan was already set in motion whereby the earth would be returned to its rightful owners through the redemption which would be provided by the death of the spotless Lamb.

Just The Facts!

READ REVELATION 5

1. As John looks upon the scene in heaven, what item of great significance does he see? v. 1

2. What was required for the scroll to be opened and its seals to be loosed? v. 2

    a. Who was worthy, according to verse 3 and what was John's reaction to this discovery?

3. John was told by one of the elders to stop weeping because there *was* someone worthy to open the scroll and loose its seals. Who was that, according to verse 5?

4. John was told that a Lion was worthy to open the scroll, but when he looked, what did he see? v. 6

   a. Describe the Lamb that John saw.

   b. Revelation 13:8 gives us more insight into this "Lamb that was slain." What does it tell us?

5. Share the reaction of those around the throne when the Lamb took the scroll out of the hand of Him who sat on the throne. vv. 7-9a

   a. What was the intent of their song?

6. How many voices did John hear around the throne proclaiming the worthiness of the Lamb? v. 11

   a. What did these voices ascribe to the Lamb? v. 12

7. Exactly who did John hear speaking blessing over Him who sits on the throne and the Lamb? v. 13

   a. What were these ones saying?

REVELATION 5

Making It Personal

1. Do your best to share why Jesus, the Lion of the tribe of Judah and the Lamb that was slain before the foundation of the world, was the only one worthy to open the scroll and loose its seals. (You may see Exodus 12 and 1 Peter 1:18-19 to add to your answer.)

2. We see the 24 elders with bowls of golden incense, which we are told are the prayers of the saints. What do you realize about *your* prayers from this scene?

3. What did the 24 elders use their harps to do? What kind of a song did they sing? Why was it a *new* song?

4. According to the new song, what had the Lamb accomplished in regard to mankind?

Do you get it that *everyone* was singing, praising and worshiping God the Father and the Lamb, Jesus Christ? (See verses 8, 11, and 13.)

5. How blessed are you when you realize that there is someone who has been found worthy to redeem you from your poverty due to sin?

REVELATION 6

As we consider the sorrows that begin to manifest themselves as the seals are opened, one at a time, we can only imagine the sorrow produced in the Father's heart. He would have done it differently if it could have been that way. He provided His Son so that the world could be redeemed, but those for whom He came rejected Him. In Deuteronomy 30, the invitation was given by Moses, "See, I have set before you today life and prosperity, and death and adversity; ... So choose life" (verses 15, 19). By and large the world chose death and adversity. Now the world would have to go through the judgment period that had been prophesied through the word of the Lord, who knew what it would take to reclaim the earth and finalize redemption. And so the sorrows begin.

Just The Facts!

READ REVELATION 6

1. The first four seals brought with them the four horsemen of the apocalypse. Share to the best of your understanding what each broken seal unleashed.

   a. First Seal (vv. 1-2)

   ✤ What did John hear?

   ✤ What did John see?

   ✤ What was the effect on the earth?

   b. Second Seal (vv. 3-4)

   ✤ What did John hear?

   ✤ What did John see?

   ✤ What was the effect on the earth?

REVELATION 6

    c. Third Seal (vv. 5-6)

      ✣ What did John hear?

      ✣ What did John see?

      ✣ What was the effect on the earth?

    d. Fourth Seal (vv. 7-8)

      ✣ What did John hear?

      ✣ What did John see?

      ✣ What was the effect on the earth?

2. What did John see when the fifth seal was opened? v. 9

    a. What would we call these people?

    b. What question did they ask?

    c. What was the answer?

3. Share the incredible physical effects that transpired when the sixth seal was opened. vv. 12-14

    a. What did the people who were alive at that time do in reaction to these cataclysmic events?

    b. What did they say?

    c. What do their words reveal?

Making It Personal

1. Explain to the best of your ability why God will have to bring judgment upon the earth.

2. Why is knowing truth and loving truth the most important personal responsibility all of mankind has? What are you doing to make sure this is a priority in your life?

3. What, most likely, is the event described in the sixth seal?

4. We see that those who are hiding in caves and the rocks of the mountains understand what's taking place. Could they turn to Christ right then and be saved? Why do you think they don't?

REVELATION 7

Jews for Jesus! Of course there have been Jews for Jesus in the last 2000 years, but 144,000 in a moment of time? This is unprecedented! Wouldn't you love to be witness to this miracle? How will it happen? Only God knows, but that it will happen we can be sure. For just a moment, we take a step away from the unfolding of the wrath of God and witness, once again, His unfailing mercy.

Just The Facts!

READ REVELATION 7

1. Where does the event we are studying this week fall into place in regard to the seven seals?

2. What did John see, according to verse 1?

    a. What does this tell you about the power and value of angels?

3. Tell about the next angel John saw in verse 2. Where did he come from? What did he have with him? What did he say to the other angels?

4. Notice what the angel calls the ones who are to be sealed. v. 3

5. Where will their seal be placed? Will it be evident? Look at Revelation 14:1 and share what this seal might be. What contrasting seal will be given to those who worship the Antichrist? (See Revelation 13:15-18.)

6. What number did John hear of those who were to be sealed? Who exactly were they?

7. From your study, at what point in time were these 144,000 sealed?

8. What did John see next? v. 9

9. According to the elder, who were these people? v. 14

10. Describe their new state and how they will be taken care of. vv. 15-17

Making It Personal

1. Read Ezekiel 9:1-5. Who was selected to be sealed in this passage? What were they protected from, by receiving the seal?

2. Who is sealed now? Do you think it's possible that they are chosen for the same reasons that the Jews in Ezekiel were?

3. What is the relationship of the believer in Christ with the Holy Spirit (in New Testament times)? Ephesians 1:13-14

REVELATION 7

The relationship of God's people in the Old Testament with the Holy Spirit was different. You may look at 1 Samuel 10:1 and 6 in regard to the anointing of King Saul, and Psalm 51:11 in regard to King David for an understanding to that relationship.

4. Do you appreciate the gift you have been given as a New Testament believer? Share your understanding of this.

5. Explain how the sealing of the 144,000 shows God's mercy in the midst of His wrath.

6. How were the robes of the multitudes made white? How is it that blood cleansed their robes?

REVELATION 8

Silence in heaven. Everything stops. For a half-hour there is no praise, no joyous worship, just a pregnant pause as a hush falls across the heavenlies and brings a brief respite on earth. Why an interlude at this point? Because our gracious God is giving mankind a moment to consider his plight and turn to Christ before the seventh seal is opened and the trumpet judgments begin. The trumpet judgments will take place very near to the end of the Tribulation period.

Just The Facts!

READ REVELATION 8

1. What do you think the silence in heaven might have indicated to John?

2. What did John see at the breaking of the seventh seal? v. 2

    a. What, in fact, was the judgment of the seventh seal?

3. What did John see next? v. 3

    a. What happened to the incense that was mingled with the prayers of the saints? v. 4

    b. See how David considers his prayers from this same perspective in Psalm 141:1-2.

4. What did the angel do next, and what was the outcome? v. 5

REVELATION 8

5. Describe the judgment that each of the trumpets brought about:

   a. First trumpet (v. 7)

   ✤ What took place?

   ✤ What was the result?

   b. Second trumpet (vv. 8-9)

   ✤ What took place?

   ✤ What was the result?

   c. Third trumpet (vv. 10-11)

   ✤ What took place?

   ✤ What was the result?

   d. Fourth trumpet (v. 12)

   ✤ What took place?

   ✤ What was the result?

6. After the trumpet judgments fell, one in quick succession after another, what did John see and what did he hear? v. 13

   a. How was this another mark of the grace of God?

LUNCH-HOUR LESSONS

Making It Personal

1. Share your thoughts on what the silence in heaven might do for those on earth, considering all they will have been through by now (also considering the final words of chapter 6). Try to think of this from a personal standpoint—what would you think if there was suddenly a halt to everything horrific that has been taking place, with the heaviness of an ominous silence in heaven?

2. How does the picture of the incense mixed with the prayers of the saints encourage you? Are any prayers excluded here? What does that mean to you?

3. Discuss with your group what each of the trumpet judgments might actually be. Be creative and don't be afraid to share your own thoughts!

4. What does the fact that there are three "woes" spoken prior to the final three trumpet judgments indicate?

5. What do you see happening on earth at this current time that is preparing us for the events that we have studied in this chapter?

REVELATION 9

Can you imagine realizing that half of mankind is dead, and yet still refusing to repent. What would cause a man to hold out against God, even when he knows that God is judging the earth and he will be judged guilty? At this point it is only rebellion. God gives opportunity after opportunity for man to repent. And yet, as in the days of Pharaoh, man continues to harden his heart.

Just The Facts!

READ REVELATION 9

1. What warning was given before the final trumpet judgments? (See Revelation 8:13.)

    a. What did this give those on earth the opportunity to do?

2. When the fifth trumpet sounded, what did John see? Revelation 9:1

    a. What indicates that this star was a person?

    b. What does Isaiah 14:12 say that relates to this verse?

    c. Who do you think this is referring to?

3. The star is given a key to the bottomless pit. Who would have been the one to give him this key, and how does Revelation 1:17-18 reveal this?

4. What rose up out of the pit and what effect did it have? v. 2

a. What came out of the smoke? v. 3

5. From verses 3-11, describe:

    a. Their power.

    b. Their appearance.

    c. The limits of their power.

    d. Their king.

6. What did John hear when the sixth trumpet sounded? v. 13

    a. What exactly did the sounding of this trumpet bring about and what would be the result of this judgment? vv. 14-15

7. Describe the army John saw:

    a. What did they look like?

    b. What did they do that caused death?

    c. Where was their power?

8. How did the remnant of mankind respond to what was taking place?

REVELATION 9

Making It Personal

1. What do you believe about demons? Have you ever known anyone who you believe was demon possessed, or had any experience with that? Have you ever had an occasion to be tormented or harassed by what you thought was a demon?

2. What do you think about the occult? Have you had any dealings with it? Have you played with ouija boards, had your palms read, been involved in séances? If so, have you renounced that part of your life and brought it under the blood of Christ? (Even taking drugs in the past, if never repented for and renounced can leave you open to demonic influence.) If you thought it wasn't any big deal, maybe now, as you read Revelation 9 and the horrible manifestations of evil in the form of demonic spirits, it would be a good time to do so!

3. What wonderful provision of protection does God make for those who are sealed? (v. 4) Who will these people be?

4. Share your thoughts on what the judgments of the fifth and sixth plagues will actually be.

5. What is the saddest part of this chapter to your way of thinking?

6. What do you take away from the study of this chapter?

REVELATION 10

The entire book we are studying is a prophetic word from the apostle John, who recorded what he saw and what he heard as he stood in heaven and witnessed what was to come. In our chapter today, we see that there were things that he was forbidden to record. He saw them, but he was unable to write them down for us to read. What could they have been? Scripture calls them "seven thunders" which "uttered their voices." Evidently seven thunderous things were said, messages from the throne of God. John went to his death without telling what he heard. It will only be revealed as the days of judgment come about.

Just The Facts!

READ REVELATION 10

1. Describe the angel John saw coming down out of heaven. v. 1

2. What did this angel have in his hand? v. 2

    a. What posture did he take?

    b. What did he do, and what happened as a result? v. 3

    c. What direction was John given about what he heard?

REVELATION 10

3. After lifting up his voice as a roaring lion, what did this angel lift up? v. 5

   a. By whom did he solemnly swear? (Notice again, that even as he swore this, he had his right foot on the sea and his left foot on the land.)

   b. From verse 6, what did he swear?

   c. What would be finished, as the seventh angel sounded the seventh trumpet? v. 7

4. Who spoke to John about the little book? v. 8

   a. Whose voice was this? (See also 4:1 and 10:4.)

   b. What direction was John given by the voice in heaven?

5. What did the angel tell John to do with the book? v. 9

   a. What was his experience in eating the little book?

   b. What further command was given to him? v. 11

Making It Personal

1. Discuss the freedom of choice with which God created man. What is man free to do or not to do? What does free will have to do with judgment?

2. We are reading these things today—before they actually take place. There will be a day when we are gone. Consider what the generation that lives during the Tribulation will think if and when they read this Book of Revelation.

3. Although we can't add to or take away from this book, what could we add to what is left behind for that future generation?

REVELATION 11

We're in the midst of a great interlude between the sixth and seventh trumpets. Actually, it's a long parenthesis that lasts from Chapter 10 through Chapter 16. During this parenthesis, we are taken back to important events which have been taking place in heaven and on earth. In our chapter today, we go back to the beginning of the Tribulation, after the Rapture of the Church, to see what God has set in place for the continued witness of truth on the earth.

Just The Facts!

READ REVELATION 11

1. Our chapter begins with John being given a reed to use as a measuring rod. What exactly was he to measure?

    a. What was he to leave out and why? v. 2

2. Verse 3 talks about God's two witnesses. What exactly will they witness to?

    a. How long will they witness, and when will this take place?

    b. What are they called? v. 4

3. How powerful are these two witnesses? vv. 5-6

    a. Although they are not able to be harmed for the duration of their ministry, when exactly are they killed? v. 7

b. Who kills them?

4. How do the majority of the people feel about them? How do you know this?

   a. Is the beast victorious over the two witnesses? v. 11

   b. What happens after they come back to life? vv. 12-13

   c. How do the people respond to this?

5. At this point, we are brought back into the chronological sequence of judgments once again. What has happened, according to verse 14?

   a. See if you can remember what the first and second woes are.

6. From heaven's vantage point, what happens when the seventh trumpet begins to sound? vv. 15-18

7. What did John see in heaven at this time? v. 19

REVELATION 11

Making It Personal

1. Who might the two witnesses be? Use verse 6 as a part of your explanation, as well as any other Scriptures you know that relate.

2. Why do you think the majority of people hate these two witnesses and rejoice at their death?

3. Why are they so afraid when they come back to life?

4. Although the judgments aren't yet complete, as the seventh trumpet begins to sound it appears that those in heaven are rejoicing. What are they rejoicing over?

5. The ark of the covenant has been missing in action since early in Israel's history, but now we see it in the heavenly Temple! Explain of the significance of the ark of the covenant.

6. As a Christian, what is your ark of the covenant?

REVELATION 12

✤

Two great signs are seen in heaven and four personalities emerge in Revelation 12. And what an important chapter it is, for in it we are given the answer to the question of the hatred that has plagued the Jewish nation throughout history, as we trace its roots all the way back to the Garden, Eve, and the serpent.

Just The Facts!

READ REVELATION 12

1. From the following verses, name and describe the first three personalities John saw in heaven:

    ✤ First great sign. vv. 1-2

    ✤ Second great sign. v. 3

    ✤ Third personality. v. 5

2. Where was the dragon positioned, and what was he attempting to do? v. 4

    a. Was he successful? What happened to the child? v. 5

    b. What did the woman do? v. 6

3. Scholars agree that the woman is symbolic for the nation of Israel (see Genesis 37:9-10). Use the following verses to help you discern who the other two personalities are:

REVELATION 12

- The dragon—Revelation 12:9

- The child—Psalm 2:7-9; Revelation 19:11-15

4. Who did John see next and what was he doing? v. 7

   a. Who won? v. 8

   b. What was the result of their victory? v. 9

   c. What announcement was made in heaven?

5. Although this enemy caused much pain and suffering for those on earth, according to verse 11, in what two ways did they overcome him?

   a. How did they face persecution for Christ?

6. What was the reaction of the dragon when he was thrown out of heaven? v. 13 What does this mean?

   a. How did he persecute her? v. 15 (Remember who this refers to.)

   b. What did God do for the woman? vv. 14, 16

   c. Who did Satan go after when he saw that he couldn't destroy the woman?

LUNCH-HOUR LESSONS

Making It Personal

1. What would you say has been the "travail" of the woman, Israel?

2. Can you think of any examples from the Bible and from history that the dragon has tried to kill the child?

3. The conflict with Michael and his angels occurs at mid-point in the Tribulation. At this point, Satan is kicked out of heaven for good ("there was no longer a place found for them in heaven"). Describe the effect this will have to those on earth—particularly the Jews.

4. How have you been tormented by the accuser of the brethren?

5. Share how you can, in a practical way, follow the example of the overcomers in verse 11.

6. With the behind-the-scenes look this chapter gives us, explain to the best of your ability why there is anti-Semitism in our world. How important is it that you are not a part of this?

REVELATION 13

As the day for the Antichrist to appear draws close, our world is showing the signs. Timothy laid it out like this: "For men will be lovers of themselves, lovers of money, boasters, proud, blasphemers, disobedient to parents, unthankful, unholy, unloving, unforgiving, slanderers, without self-control, brutal, despisers of good, traitors, headstrong, haughty, lovers of pleasure rather than lovers of God, having a form of godliness, but denying its power" (2 Timothy 3:2-5). And that is just speaking of the character of men in the last days. The political climate of our day makes it clearer than ever that the day draws near.

Just The Facts!

READ REVELATION 13

1. In Chapter 12, John witnessed the two great signs in the sky, the Child that was born to the woman, and the war between Michael and his angels and Satan and his. As we begin Chapter 13, where does John find himself?

    a. What does he see? v. 1

    b. What does he tell us about this beast? v. 2

2. Correspond John's vision with the vision of Daniel in Daniel 7:2-8.

    a. What interpretation was Daniel given about the four beasts that emerged from the sea? Daniel 7:17-25

b. What will be the outcome of the reign of the fourth beast? Daniel 7:26-27

3. What did John notice about one of the seven heads of the beast? v. 3

   a. What was the result of this healed wound? vv. 3-4

4. According to verse 5, what will one of the talents of the beast be?

   a. How will he use this talent? v. 6

5. What other ability will be granted to the beast? v. 7

   a. How will the world at large respond to him? v. 8

   b. Who will not respond this way?

6. What word of encouragement does John give the believer? v. 10

7. Share what you learn about the second beast from verses 11-18:

   a. Where does he come from?

   b. What does he look like?

   c. List the things that he has the power to do.

REVELATION 13

Making It Personal

1. Talk about the political climate of our day and how it could be setting us up for the things we are reading about in Revelation 13.

2. See if you can define humanism (the "religion" of the Antichrist). What does God's Word say that is in direct opposition to the basic tenets of humanism? Romans 3:10

3. How do you think our acceptance of the occult and the supernatural over the last decades will set the stage for the "supernatural" workings of the Antichrist?

4. What kinds of things are being set in motion in our day that will one day prove to be the beginnings of the identification system of the mark of the Beast?

5. Compare the mark of the Beast with the sealing of the saints.

6. Talk about the Lamb's Book of Life. Is your name in it?

REVELATION 14

Just The Facts!

The visions keep coming. John keeps seeing and hearing things that are incredible to him. Some of them are wonderful. Some are awful. Some, to be sure, he wishes he hadn't seen. In our chapter this week he sees one of the wonderful things—once again he sees the Lamb. We are still in the interlude, between the sixth and seventh trumpet judgments, where key events and people in the seven year Tribulation period are presented and explained.

READ REVELATION 14

1. In verse 1, John sees the Lamb again. Where is the Lamb?

    a. Who is with Him?

    b. How are they described in verse 1?

    c. How are they further described in verses 4-5?

2. Where did the voice John heard come from? v. 2 The scene has obviously shifted. Where exactly does this scene take place? v. 3

    a. What did John hear and what was happening? vv. 2-3

3. From this point on, John will witness the ministry of six angels. What were the messages of the first three angels:

    ✢ First angel—

REVELATION 14

✟ Second angel—

✟ Third angel—

4. What was John specifically told to write in verse 13?

   a. Compare the final outcome of those who "die in the Lord" (v. 13) with those who receive the mark of the beast vv. 9-11.

5. What did John see next? v. 14 Who was this?

   a. Where did the fourth angel come from, and what did he say to "Him who sat on the cloud"?

   b. What was the result? v. 16

   c. What kind of a harvest was this?

6. Where did the fifth angel come from and what did he possess?

7. Describe the sixth angel and where he came from. v. 18

   a. What did he direct the fifth angel to do?

   b. What kind of a harvest was this? v. 19

Making It Personal

1. The description in verse 4 of the 144,000 reveals that these were a special group of chosen men. Talk about the righteous lives these men lived—sharing a little bit about each aspect of their righteousness. Were these men perfect? Is it possible for us to live a life comparable to theirs?

2. What do you think their "new song" was about?

3. Have you ever sung a "new song" to the Lord after facing a severe testing of your faith? Look at Isaiah 42:9-10a in this context. What kind of a "new song" might you sing to your deliverer?

4. Think about it: Angels flying in heaven giving the gospel message and implicit words of warning to all of mankind in a way they can hear with their ears and even understand in their language. What option is God giving man? (Compare, in particular, the message of the first and third angel.)

5. Think about some of the ways God evangelizes the earth during the seven year Tribulation period. What does this reveal about our God?

REVELATION 15

This chapter represents the last of the pauses (or interludes) within the record of the judgments on "those who dwell on earth." The interludes represent the time in which God gives pause to the horrors of judgment in order for man to reflect on what has occurred. Each one marks the grace of God who is "not willing that any should perish but that all should come to repentance" (2 Peter 3:9). As we enter into the activities of Chapter 15, the last of the gracious interludes, we come to the end of grace and the beginning of the final wrath of God.

Just The Facts!

READ REVELATION 15
1. We are told in verse 1 that John saw "another sign." What kind of a sign was this one? v. 19

    a. What was the first part of the sign? v. 1

    b. What are we told about the wrath of God in this verse?

2. What else did John see at this time? v. 2

    a. Where did we see this same scene in Revelation before? What is the difference this time? (Revelation 4:6)

3. What song were these victorious ones singing?

   a. What type of song is this?

   b. What does the last line in the song reveal?

4. What did John see next? v. 5

   a. Describe those who came out of the Temple.

5. We are told that the seven angels had the seven plagues. What would these seven plagues actually be? (You may see both Revelation 8:13 and 10:7.)

   a. Although they hold the seven plagues, what are they given by one of the four living creatures?

6. What filled the temple at this point?

   a. What was the result?

REVELATION 15

Making It Personal

1. In John's vision, he sees those who have gotten the victory over the beast, his image, and his mark (v. 2). Consider the person reading this chapter during the Tribulation. What might this verse and the truth it represents do for them? In other words, what would they learn from this verse that would bring them courage and hope?

2. How did these people overcome? Revelation 12:11

3. John hears them singing the song of Moses and the song of the Lamb. Share briefly about the deliverance of Israel, led by Moses. What type of deliverance did Jesus, the Lamb bring about? How important are these events in the history of God's people?

4. John sees the "temple of the tabernacle of the testimony in heaven." Talk about what the Temple was used for in the past.

5. What happened in the Temple when Christ was crucified? (See Mark 15:37-38.)

6. Why is the Temple in heaven open now? (See Hebrews 10:19-22.)

7. Share what this means to you personally.

REVELATION 16

And so we come to the beginning of the end, as the seven angels pour out their golden bowls of wrath one by one in quick succession. Chapter 16 brings us back into the chronological order of judgments—recording, in order, the events that bring about the end of the world as we know it.

Just The Facts!

READ REVELATION 16

1. Answer the following questions about the pouring out of the seven bowls of wrath:

   a. First bowl (v. 2)

   ✠ Where was this bowl poured out?

   ✠ What was the plague?

   ✠ Who, specifically, was affected by this plague?

   b. Second bowl (v. 3)

   ✠ Where was this bowl poured out?

   ✠ What was the plague?

   ✠ How many living things died?
   c. Third bowl (v. 4)

   ✠ Where was this bowl poured out?

   ✠ What was the plague?

   ✠ What justification was given for this particular plague?

REVELATION 16

d. Fourth bowl (v. 8)

✠ Where was this bowl poured out?

✠ What was the plague?

✠ What was the reaction of mankind to this plague?

e. Fifth bowl (v. 10)

✠ Where was this bowl poured out?

✠ What was the plague?

✠ Make sure to notice who, specifically, was affected by this plague. What was their reaction?

f. Sixth bowl (v. 12)

✠ Where was this bowl poured out?

✠ What was the result of this bowl of wrath?

✠ For what purpose was this work of God done?

✠ What else did John see at this point? (v. 13)

✠ What was the result? (v. 14)

✠ Where were these gathered? (v. 16)

g. Seventh bowl (v. 17)

✠ Where was this bowl poured out?

✠ What did John hear, as this bowl was poured out?

✠ From each of these verses, what was the result of this bowl being poured out: vv. 18, 19, 20, and 21?

LUNCH-HOUR LESSONS

Making It Personal

1. Several of the bowl judgments correspond to the plagues sent upon Pharaoh and Egypt when his heart was hardened and he refused to let God's people go. Scan Exodus 7-11 and note the similarities in the plagues that were sent then and now.

2. We see on several occasions in Exodus, that the Israelites and their property are specifically protected from the plagues that pummel Egypt. (See Exodus 9:4, 26; 10:23; 11:7.) Do you see any similarity for the believers who are alive during the plagues of Revelation 16? What word would this speak to those who are affected by these plagues?

3. What are your thoughts on the similarity of God's judgments on Egypt in Moses' day and His judgments on the world during the seven years of Tribulation? (Consider why these judgments occurred, who God was judging, who God was delivering, and the heart condition of those being judged.)

4. Even in the midst of the worst destruction man has even known, there is a word of hope. What is it? (v. 15) Who would this word have been written for? What would this do for them?

REVELATION 17

At this point, once again, the events we read about are taken out of chronological order, as John takes us back to explain the "why" of some of the most awful judgments that will take place. In Chapters 17-18 we will be shown systematically how Jesus gains victory over the beast and his kingdom. We saw in Revelation 16, in the final bowl judgment, that Babylon is given "the cup of the wine of the fierceness of His wrath" (verse 19). In Revelation 17:1, John is bid to come and observe the judgment of "the great harlot who sits upon many waters."

Just The Facts!

READ REVELATION 17

1. The angel in verse 1 is going to show John why the great harlot will be judged. How does he describe her in verses 2-3?

   a. The impression here is that the harlot reigns over the many waters. Later John is told what the water she sits on represents. What is it? v. 15

2. To understand the nature of the judgment and who/what is being judged, John is taken to another place. Where is he taken and in what manner? v. 3a

   a. Here John sees a woman sitting on a beast. Describe both the woman and the beast from the following verses:

   ✣ Verse 3—the beast

   ✣ Verses 4—the woman

b. What name was written on the woman's forehead?

c. John saw that the woman was drunk. With what was she drunk? v. 6

3. What does the angel tell John about the beast? v. 8a

   a. Consider what has happened to someone who was, and is not, and yet is. Why will the people marvel? Why won't believers marvel?

4. The seven heads on the beast represent two things. What is the first? v. 9

   a. What else are we told the seven heads on the beast represent? v. 10

   b. The beast not only has the seven heads that represent these kings and kingdoms, but what amazing thing are we told about him in verse 11?

5. John is told in verse 12 that the ten horns are ten kings. What does verse 13 tell us about these ten kings?

   a. Who will they make war with, and what will be the outcome? v. 14

6. Although up until now we've had the impression that the beast and the harlot are working in unison, what are we told in verse 16? What does this mean?

REVELATION 17

    a. Why will this happen? v. 17

7. Verse 18 tells us that the woman is "that great city which reigns over the kings of the earth." What city do you think this is?

Making It Personal

1. This is a difficult chapter to interpret, but let's try! Let's begin by looking at the woman (as we will be considering the beast more in our next study). The woman is called a harlot. What is a harlot?

2. In the Old Testament, idolatry—the worship of other gods (in other words false worship and false religion) was often spoken of as adultery. The prophet Hosea was actually directed by God to take a wife who would be unfaithful to him, just as Israel had been unfaithful to God, as an object lesson to Israel. How does Hosea 3:1 reveal that God equates adultery to worship of other gods?

3. In contrast to harlotry, Jesus desires a pure bride. How does 2 Corinthians 11:2 say this?

4. If the true Church is removed when the Rapture happens, what will the harlot be?

5. Discuss the difference between having a true relationship with Christ and merely following a religious system..

REVELATION 18

The seven heads on the beast in Revelation 17 represent seven kingdoms—five that were, one that is, and one that is still to come. The "one that *is*," at the time John wrote this book, was the Roman Empire, the sixth of the kingdoms represented by the heads of the beast. It appears that it is this sixth kingdom that will come back in a revived form to be the kingdom the seventh head represents. We might look at it this way: the sixth head is the Roman Empire phase one; the seventh head is the Roman Empire phase two.

Last week we looked at the judgment of the false religion that permeates the seven years of Tribulation. This week we will see the demise of the economic system of the end-times. And here is the good news: The judgment of Babylon is the final event before the coming of Christ!

Just The Facts!

READ REVELATION 18

1. *"After these things"*—the events of Chapter 17 and in particular the judgment of the harlot—what does John see next? Revelation 18:1

    a. The angel makes an important announcement. Who has fallen, according to this angel's words?

    b. How does the angel describe the fallen Babylon? v. 2

    c. List the next three statements he makes about Babylon. v. 3

2. What was the next voice that John heard? v. 4

REVELATION 18

    a. Who is speaking here, and who is this announcement meant for?

    b. Because her sins had reached heaven and God remembered her iniquities, what was going to transpire for her? vv. 6-7a

3. Verse 7 talks about the pride of this evil world system. What is the self-perception of this world government of the Antichrist?

    a. How will the judgment come, according to verse 8?

    b. What will be the response of the rulers of the world? vv. 9-10

4. Why do the merchants weep and mourn over the demise of this world power. v. 11

    a. Make a list of some of the things that brought wealth to these grieving merchants.

    b. How does verse 14 describe the loss?

    c. Where do the merchants position themselves, and what do they say? vv. 15-16

5. Who else mourns over the loss of the great city? vv. 17-19

a. What is heaven's response to these things? vv. 20-21

b. According to verses 22-23, list the things that will not be "heard" or "found" in Babylon anymore.

c. In the end, what was Babylon's legacy? v. 24

Making It Personal

1. What (actually who) is the dwelling place of God, according to Ephesians 2:22? Whose dwelling place is Babylon? (v. 2)

2. We think sometimes that God is never going judge the evil in this world. What have you learned in your study of Revelation about the truth of that?

3. Do you remember the stock market crash of 1929? How might that scenario help you understand the possibility of an entire world system falling in a single hour?

4. How might the country's (and even the world's) response to the crash of the stock market be a modern-day example of the world's great lamentation over the fall of the great and almighty (or so they thought!) Babylon?

REVELATION 19

How great will the response in heaven be to the reality that Babylon is fallen? To understand that we must understand what Babylon really represents. We are warned all through Scripture to beware of false religion and false gods, but do we really get it? False religion, in whatever forms it takes—whether occultism, humanism, cultism, or even that which calls itself "Christianity" but is really only flesh-driven "religion"—keeps people from a true relationship with Jesus Christ. Think of all the people who will not be in heaven, even though they "believed" that they knew the true God but instead were partakers of the lie of Satan, and the false god/gods he sold them. And then think of the blood that has been shed because Satan led those who were following the religious system he set in motion to torture and kill the true followers of Christ. Will there be great rejoicing in heaven when the great harlot who was corrupting the earth is judged? You bet there will, and in our chapter this week the rejoicing begins!

As we begin in Revelation 19, all who are in heaven respond to the great reality of Babylon's fall in a multitude of magnificent choruses of praise to God!

Just The Facts!

READ REVELATION 19
As we begin in Revelation 19, all who are in heaven respond to the great reality of Babylon's fall in a multitude of magnificent choruses of praise to God!

1. What was their next reason to rejoice? v. 7

    a. What are we told about the bride in verse 8? What does the bride wear to the wedding?

    b. What was John told to write about this marriage supper of the Lamb? v. 9

2. What incredible thing does John next? v. 11?

3. From the following verses, describe Jesus as John sees Him at this time.

    ✟ Verse 12

    ✟ Verse 13

    ✟ Verse 15

    ✟ Verse 16

4. Who is with Jesus as He returns to earth ready for battle? v. 14

5. There are two suppers in Revelation 19. The marriage supper of the Lamb, and the one we find in verse 17. Who is invited to *this* supper?

    a. What will this feast be comprised of? v. 18

6. From verses 14a and 19a, describe the scene of the battle: who was fighting against whom? Did those described in verse 19a have any chance?

    a. How will Jesus fight this battle? v. 15

7. Describe the result of this battle of the beast, the kings of this earth and their armies, and the true and faithful Jesus Christ. vv. 20-21

REVELATION 19

Making It Personal

1. In heaven, God's judgment was found to be true and righteous. Would the people on earth who are being judged agree with heaven's assessment? What is God's judgment found to be by those who deny His Lordship (think about people you know personally who don't believe in the Deity of God)?

2. All the while the judgments were being poured out over the earth, there was a secret meeting taking place in heaven. It was the Judgment Seat of Christ, where those who had been Raptured stood before Christ to have their Christian service judged. It is here that we will be made ready for the marriage supper of the Lamb. See 1 Corinthians 3:13-15 and share your best understanding of what this judgment actually is.

3. Are you serving Christ out of duty or out of love? Are you serving in the flesh (perhaps as a way of earning God's approval) or are you leaning entirely upon His Spirit for the work you do in the body of Christ? These are important things to take to heart while you are still in a place to get it right! Be honest with yourself, and make the appropriate heart and mind changes so that you will be rewarded on that day!

4. We see in this chapter several names of Jesus. Throughout the Book of Revelation, there are many more given. From each of the following verses, write the name, title, or description given Jesus. (In some of these verses there are several names given—see if you can get them all!) Enjoy! Revelation 1:5, 8, 17, 18; 2:18; 3:7, 14; 5:5; 13:8; 19:11, 13, 16; 22:16

REVELATION 20

Two great and awesome events take place in Revelation 20—two resurrections. One we rejoice over, the other should bring us to tears. Revelation 19 ended with the Beast and the False Prophet being cast alive into the Lake of Fire. Our chapter this week begins with the confinement of Satan for 1,000 years, during which time Christ and the saints will reign, and the earth will be free of his deception.

Just The Facts!

READ REVELATION 20

1. Revelation 20:1 resumes the chronological order of events. We have read all through John's account, "I heard," and "I saw." What does John see now? v. 1

    a. What did the angel do with the chain? v. 2

    b. What did he do with the key? v. 3a

2. We see that Satan will be rendered powerless at this time. What will he be unable to do? v. 3b

    a. What will happen at the end of this period of time?

3. Describe the amazing things John saw next from verse 4:

    ✣ Who was seated on the thrones—what had happened to them?

    ✣ What privilege were they given?

REVELATION 20

4. What is this "life-giving" event called? v. 5

    a. What are those involved in this event called, in verse 6?

    b. Why?

    c. What privilege will these be given?

5. Now John sees even further into future history—as the 1,000 years are completed. What happens at the end of that time? vv. 7-8a (Notice who Satan is able to gather into war against God.

    a. Describe the final battle between good and evil—who wins? v. 9

    b. What is the final outcome for Satan? v. 10

6. What is the next vision of John? v. 11

    a. Who, exactly, is there in this scene? v. 11-13

    b. What is taking place?

    c. What is the horrible outcome of this event and what is its name? v. 14

Making It Personal

1. What will you be doing during the Millennium? See if you can think of what this might look like.

2. Just how wonderful do you think it would be to live in a time when Satan the deceiver was bound? Describe the difference it would make in the life of a believer.

3. 1,000 years is a long time. What will happen during these years that will provide Satan fertile ground for his evil plans when he is released? (See verse 8.)

4. See if you can describe what will take place at the great white throne of judgment (vv. 12-15). See Matthew 25:31-46

   a. What do the men and women know when God is through opening the books?

REVELATION 21

In our last chapter we saw heaven and earth flee away in the presence of God on His great white throne. This week there is a new heaven and a new earth! The new world has come! Although this is future to us, it is a certainty on which we can and should build our hope. After all the difficult things we have read in this book, we now come to the place of great rejoicing!

Because the description of the New Jerusalem continues into the first five verses of Chapter 22, we will be looking at Revelation 21-22:5 in our study this week.

Just The Facts!

READ REVELATION 21-22:5

1. What amazing vision does John describe for us in verse 1?

2. What does John call the New Jerusalem? v. 2

    a. Where does it come from?

    b. How has it been prepared by God?

3. Next John hears a great announcement. What is he told in verse 3?

4. More precious information about this time is given in verse 4. List the "no mores" of this verse.

    a. Give three reasons why these things will be no more. vv. 4b, 5a, 6a

5. Who is speaking to John in verse 6 and how does He describe Himself?

   a. What does God promise to give the one who thirsts?

6. Who will be the recipient of all that God has prepared? v. 7

   a. Who will be absent from this glory? v. 8

7. When the angel says to John, "Come, I will show you the bride, the Lamb's wife" (verse 9), where does he take him and what does he show him? v. 10

   a. Make a list describing the glorious city from Revelation 21:11-21 and Revelation 22:1-2.

8. Now, from Revelation 21:22-27 and Revelation 22:3 make a list of the things that will not be there and why they will be missing.

9. To add to all the amazing things we have learned in these chapters, we are given two more facts that place the finishing touch upon the picture. What does Revelation 22:4 tell us about ourselves in that day?

   a. What will we be doing for eternity? Revelation 22:5

REVELATION 21

Making It Personal

1. What does it mean to you that you will "dwell with God"?

2. Verse 4 tells us that the former things will have passed away. From the context of this verse and beyond (use your imagination, thinking of the reality of the world we live in now), what are some of those things?

3. This record tells us that God will wipe away every tear from our eyes. What does Psalm 56:8 reveal that goes along with this thought? Consider some of the tears He will wipe away from *your* eyes.

4. Go back over the verses that describe the physical appearance of the New Jerusalem—Revelation 21:11-21. Use your imagination to really picture this city. Do you see it? What does it look like to you? Which aspect of it excites you the most?

REVELATION 22

Who may come? "Whosoever will" (Revelation 22:17 KJV). This has been the invitation throughout all of Scripture and it is that word that finishes the revelation of our Lord, who is "not willing that any perish but that all should come to repentance" (1 Peter 3:9).

And so we come to the end of the Book of Revelation. What an amazing unveiling it has been! As we finish, may we join with John in saying, "Even so, come, Lord Jesus!" (Revelation 22:20).

Just The Facts!

READ REVELATION 22:6-21

1. Who gave John this revelation and why was it given? See also Revelation 1:1.

2. What is the testimony of Jesus at this point? v. 7

    a. What is John's testimony about what he has written? v. 8a

3. What word of instruction does the angel give John about the words of this book and why? v. 10 What does the Lord obviously want us to do with these words?

4. Verse 11 is a little bit difficult. Considering that it follows the words "for the time is at hand." Could it be a warning? How does a person who remains in his sin, in light of all the Lord has offered, confirm the fact that he is a sinner condemned to the Lake of Fire? Will there be a second chance for those who die in their sin?

REVELATION 22

    a. What encouragement might verse 11 be to the one who has lived in light of the Scriptures, but is still awaiting the Lord's return?

5. In verse 12, Jesus repeats for the second time in this chapter that He is coming quickly. What is He going to bring with Him for His servants and what is the "qualifier" for this?

    a. Do you think this speaks of quantity of work? What does it speak of?

6. How does Jesus make it clear that these words written by John are from Him? v. 16

7. What is the message of verse 17?

    a. What universal invitation is given in this verse?

8. How important are the words of this testimony? vv. 18-19

9. Once again, for the third time in this chapter, Jesus says, "Surely I am coming quickly" (verse 20). What is John's response?

    a. Is this your response?

10. What is the final note of John to the words of this revelation? v. 21

Making It Personal

1. From Revelation 1:3 and 22:7, just how important does God consider the words of this prophecy for the believer? What does that mean to you? What does that mean to the church?

2. Verses 18-19 also reveal the seriousness of God about the words of this book. You and I wouldn't knowingly add to or take away from these words, but what might we (or perhaps a preacher) do?

3. What is the request of the Holy Spirit and the bride in verse 17 and John in verse 20? Who is this word directed to? Is this word in your heart, as you see the day approach?

4. What is the great and final invitation to the one who is thirsty (verse 17)? What do the words "whosoever will" mean to you?

5. Share how your study on the Book of Revelation has changed you.

ABOUT THE AUTHOR

Linda has dedicated her life to serving the Lord as a teacher, writer, and speaker. While teaching the Word of God, training leaders, and speaking at retreats and other women's ministry functions, she has also written curriculum for over 20 books of the Bible.

If you would be interested in having more information about her ministry, please visit her blog at www.lindaoborne.wordpress.com, or email her at myutmost1@aol.com.

www.ingramcontent.com/pod-product-compliance
Lightning Source LLC
Chambersburg PA
CBHW071412040426
42444CB00009B/2209